This time called life

—Walter Rinder

CELESTIAL ARTS
Millbrae, California

First Printing, October, 1971

Made in the United States of America

Library of Congress Card No.: 75-174240
ISBN: 0-912310-05-7

7 8 9 10 11 12 – 80 79 78 77

Dedication

To the young people of
"This Speck of Earth"
Gallery, Portland, Oregon . . .
whose lives helped to weave the
emotional and visual blanket of this book.

You have added a multitude of
experiences to my life . . . I have grown.

—Walter Rinder

Walter Rinder

About the author

Yesterday

My name is Walter Murray Rinder ... Gemini by the stars.

My youth was spent in Southern California, not too far from the seashore. When I wasn't working in our yard planting flowers (watching things grow), I liked to be with my friends.

My folks are wonderful people. They never taught me who I should be, they guided me to myself. They had a lot to give and they gave.

I went to college and studied many things ... learned a lot more about life from traveling in my country and reading books and listening to people.

I've lived many ways of life, meeting many different types of people. They were all beautiful if I took the time to allow their beauty to flow.

Of the many places I've lived, I call San Francisco my home. That city, more than any place, showed me life ... naked.

Today

Now I live in Portland, Oregon. I have a Photography Gallery and craft shop called "This Speck of Earth, filled with beautiful young people.

Tomorrow

I will travel all over the world ... learning, loving and sharing with you my life.

What
we
call
life

We arrive in this world alone . . . this time called
life was meant to share.

Under the cover of the stars,
under the cover of the sun fermented into eternity
there lies a precious moment of time we call life.
A gift of Creation.
We are given minds to discover,
talent to create,
curiosity to gain knowledge,
insight to build,
emotions to communicate our feelings,
and movement through our physical body.

Open your gift!

Close to earth

Close to the earth
where the wind blows free
a man sets down roots
for his children to see

They learn from the deer
Its swiftness in flight
They learn from the bear
Its strength and its might

They learn from the bird
Its grace and its songs
They learn from the snake
Where they don't belong

They learn from the flowers
Their colors and smells
They learn from the waters
To seek their own wells

As the seasons pass by
a man in his toil
knows that his children
Have learned from the soil

Their hearts filled with love
Their spirit unchained
His children aren't sculptured
with fear or with pain

Close to the earth
where the wind blows free
a man sets down roots
for his children to see

Aura
of
life

Winters aura
brings the snow
also makes the fires glow

Springs young aura
brings new birth
also shows a man his worth

Summers aura
brings the sun
sends its children on the run

Autumns aura
brings the wind
that makes the leaves gaily spin

All the seasons
bring balanced strife
to make us conscious of our life

Sometimes I feel like a bird

Sometimes I feel like a
bird
free in its flight,
but constantly aware
of looking for a place to rest;
searching for food to fill
the hunger within. And in my
freedom of movement, like the
bird,
we both are creatures of needs.
        They must be fulfilled.

Raindrops

1.

Slender needles of the pine
From the branches sway
To hold the beauty of the clouds
Tiny raindrops come to stay

2.

Raindrops are only . . . tiny mirrors
hanging from branches
emulating our reflection
in truth
bringing us closer
to life

Caring

I care about you in a troubled wind
when you find it hard to hold on
              your dreams blow away
              your hopes don't seem to stay
my strength stands with you till the calm

I care about you in our city's jungle
when you're afraid because you've lost your way
              when the loneliness entwines
              the fragile web of your mind
I'll show you a path, then I'll stay

I care about you in the games people play
when you've played the best you can
              for when people cheat
              or you are constantly beat
with my caring we'll win the next hand

Pain

When a child is born of woman,
she feels his pain.
The child being born,
she forgets the pain,
feeling only the love of her labor.

So be it with youth . . .
growing up feeling the pain
of their conditioning.
When the knowledge of love
is born unto themselves,
they forget the pain,
feeling only the truth of their labor.

I
asked
God

I asked God to help me find love

He told me, You are love

I asked God to help me find a purpose

He told me "You are the purpose"

I asked God to help me find truth

He told me "You are truth"

Then God said

"When you find me

your questions will cease"

Remember the good times

at the sea

when we tore our shells away, our emotions
poured forth — lying in the sand, your head
resting on my chest, you listening to the
impatient beating of my heart — or me to yours.

with the sky

when we ran down the hills to the rhythm
of the clouds, laughing at the rain, kissing
your wet lips, crying because of our
overabundance of happiness.

in the mountains

beneath the waterfall where we made our
commitment, to stay together forever
I truly believe we meant it then.

Life constantly changes reality

Did we dwell too long under the spell of love's dreams?
Were we hypnotized not to move with the essence of life?
Did our love drift apart by the turbulance of the
                          winds of change?

goodbye

remember the good times

One
life

There are countless paths of knowledge
There are many ways to give
There are endless hopes to dream of
There is only one life for us to live

Don't waste your time in sorrow
jealousy or pain
pity envy depression
or things that are the same

Every year that we get older
more often you hear people say
I wished I would have, I should have done
I just wasted another day.

Poetry
of the
eyes

*They search beyond the realm
of senses, into the blue stream
of beauty, drifting along as the
clouds reflection.*

A life unfolds.

A life of longing

I've
still
got
me

Autumn strips the trees, to send the leaves away
Winter covers grass, where I once used to play
Spring melts the snow, round the cabin that was my home
Summer breath whispers, go my son it's time to roam

I've still got me.

I sit by my window, with the fog draped moon
Remembering my footsteps, traveling the minstrel's tune
To the places I knew, when back I went
Finding them changed, in the time I spent

I've still got me.

So I'll just jump on the carousel and ride
on the horse to the post, who is always tied
For as we circle, and life whizzes by
It's the blur of the lonely, I watch who cry

I've still got . . .

me.

Four days of life

Experiencing
Feeling
Understanding
Change

I saw life through the eyes of a child
as I watch him clean his boat
before putting it into the lake.
      We can learn from children.

Now
that
we have
touched

1.

Now that we have touched, where do we go
from here? Why must actions be only moments?
The stagnant pond omits life.
You know non-movement can do that,
just sitting still!

2.

Is it my silence you fear the most or
my actions. If I move freely within
myself, you draw away and begin to run.
Come back!

3.

I met a human being; we shared many hours together.
He said as he left that evening, "I'll see you
around sometime." He never even knew my name!

4.

My folks and I are worlds apart, yet we are close
within the heart. When I go home, their world is
strange, only because it is I who has changed.
They are happy. Am I?

Friends

I became friends with a chipmunk
giving him bits of bread
He received by taking them.

What a pleasure.

Night passage

In a crowded coffee shop late at night two strangers
met with their eyes. A story unfolds; searching
each others mind for a glimmer of understanding.
The young fellow's eyes staring from a gaunt
face, expressionless, as if the eyes were
set apart in space. Yet his eyes held the
moment of conception between the mind and the
body, waiting birth, when the baby left on the
unknown doorstep will be found and lifted by
the caring arms of a human being. His eyes were
pleading, but the older stranger was too preoccupied
with his own self to see the story, only darting
moments of non-relating.

As the man left, their eyes met for the last time,
the younger eyes open wide crying to be lifted
from the doorstep. The man's eyes replied I have
no arms to lift you, my son.

Can't you see?

It was cold outside as I walked to my car.

Spending time

1.

He had one arm . . . one leg
nineteen, I think
he smiled at me
I returned the smile
he smiled at someone else
they turned away

2.

Long hair covers the face when the
wind is blowing.
Once on a windy day I watched people
not seeing each other.
Cities are very windy!

3.

Can we say with our lips what our hands
say
let my lips in silence say I love you
See our shadow on the wall!

4.

I feel caged as I look through the tattered window
shade at the neon sign blinking. I in a strange room
in a strange city. How many lonely people such as I
have laid on this bed. Was it ever shared by two!

5.

She was with a crowd of kids running along the
beach. I was alone walking barefoot in the water.
As they passed me, she came over and hugged me .
saying, "Have a beautiful day"
She took the time!

Growth

His love was . . . simple, uninhibited
child like, spontaneous
filled with touching, giving roses
poetry
he never grew up . . .
thank God!

Artists and craftsmen open
the door to beauty.
Let us enter

Fullness of love

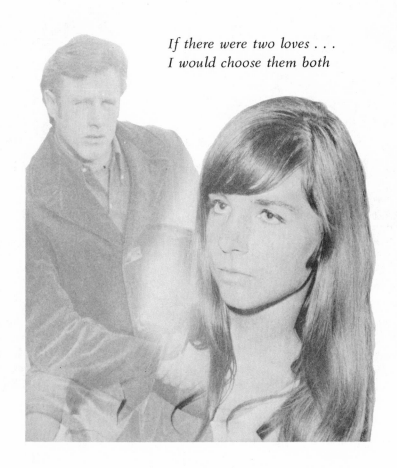

If there were two loves . . .
I would choose them both

The
bridge

my friend,

I have built a bridge for you

to cross over to me . . .

but not a vehicle

to carry you

Of
a friend,
I say

A friend is

someone with whom you can share your thoughts
without fear . . .
of his walking away in condemnation
seeking his understanding

A friend is
someone with whom you can be naked in body
without fear . . .
of ridicule or rejection of your imperfections
seeking his harmony

A friend is
someone with whom you can probe his soul
without fear . . .
of your acceptance
seeking his knowledge

A friend is
someone with whom you can lie next to and hold
without fear . . .
of his attitude toward your intentions
seeking his warmth

A friend is
someone with whom you can plan time to share
without fear . . .
of his indifference
seeking his honor

A friend is
in truth a human being
there is no fear . . .
your life, which is precious, is shared
seeking your peace

Understanding

Raindrops never care to stay
nor clouds on passing by
or will rainbows let you touch them
as they arch upon the sky

A waterfall is never still
nor leaves in autumn season
or wind that bends the marsh grass down
that gives no apparent reason

Our footsteps trod on many paths
beneath the cover of the sky
for man has shown by living
we find the reasons, why

Travel far, my weary friend
with nature's careful planning
touch the flowers of the soul
then wait, for understanding

" I'm
a boy
you
see "

I once knew a man
Who felt love for me
But I couldn't return it
For I'm a boy, you see.

Our society has taught me
What is right, what is wrong
I'm conditioned I know
Oh God! for how long.

> *Will I die a boy to be a man*
> *Will my soul fly free, or sink in the sand*

The sound of his words
The feel of his touch
It is fear that I feel
Though I love him so much.

Why when we lay
So close in the night
The division between us
Brings together our plight.

> *Will I die a boy to be a man*
> *Will my soul fly free, or sink in the sand*

"I love you", he'd say
"No shame do I hold
For my feelings are natural
It's the world that is cold."

His thoughts were like spears
Cast deep in my heart
For the world it has taught me
I should have no part

Of his touch or affection
Of his wanting to give
I'm being pulled apart
By this life that I live

> *Will I die a boy to be a man*
> *Will my soul fly free, or sink in the sand*

Love is the answer
I know, oh I know!
But How do I show Him
When fear rules me so

I toss and I turn
I stumble, I fall
I spin like a top
Till it hits the wall

My brain, it's exploding
My feelings need air
It's an unnatural life
When people don't care

> *Will I die a boy to be a man*
> *Will my soul fly free, or sink in the sand.*

When will I open
My love for this man
Being proud and happy
To take hold of his hand

I once knew a man
Who felt love for me
But I couldn't return it
For I'm a boy, you see

> *Will I die a boy, to be a man*
> *Will my soul fly free, or sink in the sand?*

You

You pull me apart
with your morals and codes
you uproot vegetation
with your freeways and roads

You confuse simple minds
with your complexed ways
and twist natural feeling
since the birth of your days

You instigate wars
for your wealth and your gain
and your children are killed
with your weapons of pain

You're proud of technology
with its comforts and fun
while your factories pollut
the air, hiding the sun

Complacent you stand
in your houses of glass
while your people march by
destroying life as they pass

I'll no longer partake
of your malice of thought
as you repeat your mistakes
for nature has taught

That the meaning of life
is to share and to give
to build with your hands
and your minds as you live.

From
   the
      city
    we fled

From the city we fled
to snow covered mountains
The sun followed our day
exploring a magnificent world that
we might have known
but not together
sharing worlds we did know
together . . .
a small waterfall
by the road
icicles . . . sculptured
pine branches
snow in their hands
waving to us
when the wind arose
clouds by the multitudes
in wondrous patterns
as if God were painting
a canvas for us . . .
trees of pure gold
standing like sentinels
by the brooding hills
ashamed of their nakedness
in and among this we spoke
our words floated to the earth
with the snowflakes
covering the ground
the love shadows came
with night's approach
as we sat on the fence
watching the canvas completed
the painting was for us . . .

We must be strong

It is not enough that God gives us gifts of love, gifts of physical beauty, gifts of talent; for these are only a few of the pillars which are rooted in the foundation of our personality. The strength of this foundation is life. The building starts at birth. Its strength over the years, our mending the cracks replacing the parts that crumble or are weakened by time; depend on our perception, our confidence, our giving and receiving, our inter-acting with life, our sensitivity, fulfilling our commitments and honoring our word. Also the strength of this foundation depends on our understanding and overcoming hurts and pains, disappointments and failures, conditionings and fears. For these are the storms which can destroy (lay these pillars to ruins) or weaken our mind and our body.

From birth until death these storms are constantly tearing down people who can't build the strength to stand against their might. Cities are full of these people and cities are the eyes of these storms.

So many human beings lie in the rubble of their personality.

Round

Man   woman

man   man

woman   woman

all on the ferris wheel of life

paired lovers   united

married couples divided

all on the ferris wheel of life

around and around goes the wheel
faster and faster this circle of steel
concrete and asphalt go whizzing by
come ride with me as we pierce the sky

man and boy   daring
girl and woman   sharing
hippy and straight   comparing
establishment   staring
all on the ferris wheel of life
our government in   contemplation
our society in   condemnation
our police in   retaliation
our youth in   meditation . . .
rebuilding a new foundation
all on the ferris wheel of life

around and around goes the wheel
faster and faster this circle of steel
concrete and asphalt go whizzing by
come ride with me as we pierce the sky

I'm getting dizzy
let me off!

I cry

I cry when I see indifference
as a man lies in the street
people walk on by his hurts
with scared and frightened feet

I cry when on the radio
I hear the dying of young men
who traveled to some foreign land
never to see their home again

I cry when I see a young girl
engulfed in unnatural highs
as she escapes the living,
trying to find the reasons why!

I cry when I feel the heartbeat
of a lonely soul's embrace
for I know what they are feeling
I've been to that same place

I cry for earth's humanity
for its destiny may become
a void and empty planet
moving listlessly around the sun

I cry because I have the faith
so deep within my heart
that man can change the ugliness
that has always been a part

Of human movement in all times
the values have been placed
on superficial attitudes
a stigma of the human race.

Returning

He runs
                to meet the setting of the sun
                        following roads
                                to nowhere
                                somewhere
                                he doesn't care
                keep going lad, become free
                                no going back
                                back to what?
        explore
                experience
                        develop
                                change

run
        to meet the setting of the sun

Discovery

I awoke

in the time of dawn

with hope

on this new day

love would find me

Christmas Eve

*Here in the country, everyone has gone to friends or
relatives homes for their traditional Christmas and
I am left alone. But in spirit I have been given a
splendor beyond man's deepest dreams for before my
eyes is a wonderland so magnificent, so inspiring
that if there were angels they would be crying tears
of joy.*

I am surrounded by a whole forest of the most beautiful, pine scented, living Christmas trees, reaching toward the sky a hundred times taller than myself. At the tips of these trees are thousands of stars shining and twinkling and sparkling everywhere I look. All around me is an aura of Christmas music; the little stream I am sitting by is a choir of many voices singing the carols of Christmas, my two dogs running back and forth across the old wooden bridge are the sound of the cymbals and drums, every so often a night bird cries out like Christmas chimes, the wind blowing through the branches are the violins playing Silent Night, the frogs are the horns and the crickets the flutes and together they all are my symphony of Christmas, present. My Christmas is a living, real experience. Even Tom-Tom our turkey looks far more beautiful in his pen, his autumn colored feathers fanned out with such pride, than cooked sitting on the table.

God, thank you for your Christmas gifts to me and for the mistletoe high in the trees, the pine cones sitting on the branches, the red berries on the bushes, the acorns on the ground and the poinsettias growing near the barn. You have given unto me the discovery on this Christmas eve that the most valued of gifts we can give or receive is the meaning of life through the spirit of love.

Oh lonely boy

As I walked along the country road
on a peaceful winter's day
I came upon a boy alone
which fate had brought my way

With sleeping bag upon his back
an unshaven, love-worn face
he showed a friendly, youthful smile
a smile of human grace

I said to him, "Good morning lad
What is your given name
Where is it that you come from
mountains, city or distant plain?"

In tired words of certainty
he said as he sat down
"My search is long and endless
as I travel town to town

I've wandered here, I've wandered there
exploring far and wide
longing to breathe the breath of love
holding its life inside

I've been on city streets
in early morning hours
I've walked the country roads
smelling fragrant, petaled flowers

I've awakened in motel rooms
in the middle of the night
thinking all I had for company
was the conscience of my plight

I've sat upon the pilings
of a wharf where ocean flows
visioned countless human faces
in my memory of long ago

I've been in movie houses
watching lives in love and pain
my head bending on my shoulders
as the tears would fall like rain

I've met a stranger on the street
we shared the cloud filled day
but when the night bounced back again
we went our separate ways

So now you've heard my story
thank you for your time
there are many miles to cover
before nightfall rests my mind."

He arose and stood before me
reaching out to hold my hand
the last words he softly spoke
echoed loud, across our land

"Will I die a starved, unwanted boy
from the love I never find
or live my years in searching
leaving bits of me behind

Or will I find the love I need
sharing each and every day
in the beauty of togetherness
and my journey ends that way?

Sharing

we arrive upon this earth
                        alone
we depart
            alone
this time called life, was meant to share.

Home

There is a world where souls do meet
tis not upon life's busy street
but in the shelter of love's home
that our understanding cares to roam

The foundation we lay upon knowledge of truth
to hold our life up as we build our youth
we construct its strength with experienced beams
with inter-acting walls made of faith and dreams

Our roof is the depth that we can express
of our love of each other never to regress
we then build a fireplace of sharing's embrace
then light a fire for our souls to encase.

Become

*Too many people are only fragments of themselves
for others to see*

become a whole human being

The
challenge

The mountain we challenge
our destiny be
forging the cliffs
toward eternity

the north wind blows to
to spin the clouds
we try to touch above the crowds

Being

*Climb to the threshold of
your own beliefs,
not with the statement
of others,
but with the footsteps of
your own experience*

Song

Turquoise made mountains
tangerine skies
apple gold meadows
where the wizard abides

Emerald deep plains
bronze orchards shown bright
pastel colored rainbows
which give us our light

Bushes sweet laughter
trees that can walk
children that sing with
the flowers that talk

Indigo wheat fields
burnt sienna stars
a sun wrapped in silver
that seeds wisdom afar

The green pebbled path
through forests red cloak
down canyons of purple
to this wizard of oak

Clouds brushing our cheeks
waves gentle hands
thunder soft and mellow
raining amber sand

Where peace is abundant
a world — love inborn
the wizard of lovers
exiles man's bestial scorn

Where embracing is natural
kisses live free
affection glows fire
and we can just be

Journey my beloved
to my harmony land
where the wizard eternal
holds sceptre in hand

All are paired lovers
with nothing to fear
for love is the purpose
in the voices we hear.

I
need
   to be
loved

        lying upon the
blades of grass looking at your
silhouetted face
half hidden by the
night
portions lit by the
moon

your hands and mind
in motion slowly exploring my
soul and body in an aura
where time has dissolved into space

where your lips slid across my
cheeks
as the water of the
stream over
rocks

your breath hitting
me
like the wind that rushes across
us
hurrying to meet its lover

our souls, as one,
being drawn into the
whirlpool of life
deeper
we plunge into our own awareness
of each other
as night
continues its meditation

as your sounds are like the
breeze conversing with the
sentinal of pine trees
that surround us

the darkness is warm as, natural,
we are climbing the mountains of your body
walking in the quiet valleys
discovering the caverns of excitement
the beach of soft sand where, then, I rest
to float upon the ocean
of your mind

as dawn is born
of the universe's womb
sleep becomes our shroud
nature covers us with her blankets
of loves peace

when again the sun creates
the noon hour
we will arise . . .
going out into the world
projecting . . .
the spirit of loving
and being loved

as does spring
with its new buds
on the dorment trees
the melting snow
filling the dry river beds
grass turning dead hillsides
into living green carpets
new flowers, their spectrum of color
gathering together in the meadows
bringing gaiety to the lonely desert
in small groups
in the tiny pockets of cliffs

the rain of our love
to nourish other human beings
. . . in the season
of their spring . . .

Together

Wherever we are together
that be our home
for a home is where people love

Words

Words are only the
prelude
to action

Know yourself...

experience life
by crawling in its dirt and
being lifted by the wings of its beauty.

Oneness
of the
soul

Mental love is all I have shown
toward a person for this I've been taught
Physical love is morally wrong
They've implanted into my thought

Once in a while a person comes along
Whose beauty surpasses the best
Inside me arises a feeling of longing
which I hide from all the rest

Needs of love to hold and to feel
This relating, I have not yet known
I want to express this emotion I have
I fear they'll reject when it's shown

So I hide within my human shell
As a turtle when danger appears
then people won't hurt me with malice of thought
when this feeling fights to get clear

Mental love and physical love
are a oneness of the soul
I know this truth, that I must fulfill
When inside me it wants to unfold

Awareness

On a day when a man condemns me for
what I say and for my actions
may I also be sent the courage,
through my knowledge of love,
to stand before his wrath;
not in the quicksand of submission,
but on the solid rock of my own
awareness.

Precious
moments

Don't exclude yourself . . . from
precious moments
warm encounters
beautiful attitudes
majestic discoveries
flowing intimacies
sensory development

for these are the jewels
placed in the crown of your destiny

The naked moment

More often than not

caution clothed my thoughts

when I had a mind to undress

my words

I wore heavy coats in those days

It's summer now in my life

the heavy coats hang in the closet

they belong to the moths

Beyond
this
path

Beyond the curved path

across the stone arched bridge

above the etched cliff

towering high over trees

beneath the shroud of fog

. . . it began its descent

into space

cascading

free from barriers

    we stared in wonderment

no words to speak

we were learning

from its touch

there were no barriers

They are as one

Life . . . without love is like
　　　　spring without rain
　　　　love without giving is like
　　　　rain without clouds
　　　　for
　　　　　　　life
　　　　　　　　　　love
　　　　　　　　　　　　giving . . . are as one

Life . . . without faith is like
　　　　the body without exercise
　　　　faith without purpose is like
　　　　exercise without movement
　　　　for
　　　　　　　life
　　　　　　　　　　faith
　　　　　　　　　　　　purpose . . . are as one

Life . . . without knowledge is like
　　　　a tree without blossoms
　　　　knowledge without understanding is like
　　　　blossoms without seeds
　　　　for
　　　　　　　life
　　　　　　　　　knowledge
　　　　　　　　　　　understanding . . . are as one

Life . . . without discovery is like
      music without sound
      discovery without change is like
      sound without vibrations
      for
            life
                  discovery
                            change . . . are as one

Life . . . without freedom is like
      an animal without fur
      freedom without honor is like
      fur without warmth
      for
            life
                  freedom
                            honor . . . are as one

Universe . . . without life is like
      the flesh without soul
      life without people is like
      a soul without motion
      for
            universe
                  life
                            soul . . . are as one

Tidepools

You've shown me unknown worlds
on the face of leaves
under forest logs
inside ocean tidepools
within small pockets on cliffs
Yet the hidden world of my soul
still remains a mystery

Naked

He walked naked along the stream

children giggled

     laughing funny faces

people whispered

     sang their silly tunes

he was a fragment of the natural

I
am

I was born of an emotion

bursting, into the world a tear

Discard your mask!

I must stream down your face

for I am life . . .

Friend

He's companion to you when you're lonely

he's friend to you when you're blue

he's the kind that never minds

being honest, faithful and true

When you awake in the morning

and he licks the side of your face

then in the strife of a person's life

a dog has a different place

Dedicated
to my
Mom and
Dad

When you were criticizing me
and finding here and there
a fault or two to speak of
or a weakness you could tear

There are many human failures
in the average of us all
and many grave shortcomings
into which we do fall

When you were blaming me for meaness
or misunderstanding my words of truth
you remembered in this world of ours
life's not easy in our youth

I've struggled through many a sorrow
I've waded through many a fear
I've had the strength and courage
to laugh through many a tear

In my young years you had the patience
through your love to understand
building your son's self-confidence
to become a gentle man

Time

Between crevices, hued in stone
runs the waves in symphonic tones
toward the shore its destiny
from time of birth within the sea

Raining spray with joyful glee
surging forward momentously
rocks stand fast against their might
as waves leap up above the rocks height

Churning waters restless path
moves beside these rocks to laugh
waves enclose their sullen faces
sentinels standing in monotonous unchosen places

Black these giants of the shore
who in time will be no more
as boundless sea with caps of white
traveling passed in endless flight

Death awaits on yonder sand
as I watch through eyes of man
waters body twist and turn
their journey's end, I stand and learn

Art
is
long

For every philosopher

there needs to be artists

who can create visual concepts

for his thoughts . . .

placed beside the monuments of man's ego.

The city

Despondent
  depressed
    alone . . . as I walked the caverns of my city.

Chilled
  hungry
    needing . . . someone to care

                    a smile of grace
                    a gentle touch
                    a word of warmth
                    I longed for such
A young girl felt my need . . . and spoke
we walked, together, in the rain

this human being took me to her home
share tea with us, she said
share our home in love's encounter
these things I did with an open heart
while her children played on the floor
she began sewing on a frayed pillow
her young man playing his music
on a guitar with three strings broken
one of the little boys came and sat down beside me
drinking a glass of chocolate milk
the family's world filled with activity
five human beings interacting
in harmony with themselves
I caught their spirit
still I sat as a spectator
they were the participants
Her man showed me his paintings
I read some of his poetry
I listened to his words as she smiled at me
my perception of her soul
was in our moments of silence
another guitar string broke
he continued to play
life was dancing in her home
I sat remembering . . .
I sat thinking, where I would be next
passing intervals of time
in a blur of memories
I must leave now . . . to depart from her world . . . shared
going back outside into the city which was mine
Out onto the streets so my life could continue to happen.
Maybe with her and her family again or maybe with another
stranger and begin relating anew.

In memorium to Geri
who, at age 22, escaped temporarily
into drugs . . . finding death her permanent
escape

The space between life — death
  a silver thread

woven at conception — an embryo
  upon birth it strengthens
a baby — a child — its fibers grow
  with trial and error

youth holds tight, not to tumble
   precarious — this thin corridor
until perception arrives, dressed in love, saying
   I will give you assistance, youth, building
   your life upon a rock
   knowing your self worth
   developing understanding
   structuring your own respect
the thread stands firm . . .

if your choice be upon quicksand
   entirely dependent on others
   escaping in unnatural stimulants
   loss of self confidence
then your life crumbles . . .
   the thread begins to unravel

youth cries out!
   cries out!
no ears to hear, except those of death
   for the noise of humanities indifference . . .
   marches on!
   marches on!
   marching over youth's cries

The space between life — death
   a silver thread

Life
flows
free

Upon the butte he stood
sunlight filtered window shown
walls of mountains, his house enclosed
in this land, his home

sagebrush moved upon his floor
pussywillows adorned his door
gnarled scrub oak his treasured art
hawks throughout his house would dart

canyoned hallways
valleyed rooms
vases filled
with desert blooms

knowledge gained
in fossiled rocks
red winged bird
perched on hollyhocks

half moon hills
spilled amber and blue
skies constant change
into evening hue

there was a void
he knew not his worth
a time when he questioned
why of his birth

city's faded memory
confusion was gone
now life flowed free
as the rivers song

Man

MAN   creates complexities
  all else is simple
MAN   causes confusion
  all else is harmonious
MAN   breeds indifference
  all else is caring
MAN   lives in turmoil
  all else live in communion
MAN   evolves to control
  all else is free
MAN   destroys encompassing death
  all else builds toward life
MAN   distorts meaning
  all else enhances truth

MAN CONTINUES
  all else disappears

Words of enlightenment

1.

We can gain knowledge without wisdom
We cannot gain wisdom without knowledge

2.

Possess not the soul of another human being
for the abundance of your fruit may break the branch

3.

Thinking of love is life's mirage
acting in love is life's oasis

4.

It is far better to give in silence
than from the echo of your friends voice

5.

It is not by words alone that a person is revealed to us
but in our perception of his silence that we know him best

6.

Truth within us is silent
conditioning is the voice so often spoken

7.

A man can become blind

if he continues to

walk in the shadow

of his soul's own

enlightenment

8.

I give you a gift of yourself
wrapped in my love.

9.

Each man should develop the most
from the natural gifts of his body and mind
for a sense of personal achievement

10.

Loneliness can be a lack of responding
to your environment

11.

If we suspect the motive
we quite often condemn the act.

12.

Life is the endless beauty of unity.

13.

Our motives, whether honorable or fraudulent,
truly justify our actions.

14.

The stagnant pond omits life
non movement can do that
just sitting still

15.

Look for the Good in yourself
Not the evil in others.

16.

The spirit of an action or deed is far more
important than the action, for in the
intention lies the beauty or ugliness.

17.

Love can travel a thousand miles
without a sound

18.

We walk with our head looking down at the dust
instead of lifting our eyes toward the horizon

19.

Truth in one man may be folly in another
yet we carry both

20.

If a man shows you a new path in life, ask not that he walk before you, ask only if he has walked that path.

21.

Touch a human being so they may know you're there for so many are blind and deaf.

22.

Words, can keep us apart

Rivers

Rivers can only continue their motion when
water flows along their banks . . . creating
life within their essence.

I can only give that awareness I have
        inside me
You can only receive that which you are aware
        is your need.

We are rivers unto one another

Creation

Nothing of importance

or great essence

can be created unless first there are things

pre-existing.

Those things that pre-exist

become reality with the ingredient of

time,

and thought and motion in some form of

harmonious pattern.

example

A baby cannot be born without first the act of conception.

The act of conception will not materialize without first the union of intercourse.

The union of intercourse will not happen without first two human beings.

And for these to happen there are many pre-existing factors which determine a chain of events leading up to

example

Love cannot happen without first there being real actions from our senses (sight, touch, hearing, smelling, speaking, feeling from the soul)

Our senses cannot happen without first there being a need

A need cannot happen without first there being an awareness

An awareness cannot happen without first there being a thought

A thought cannot happen unless we freely allow all of life to enter our being (when the snow falls does it not cover everything, when it rains does it not touch everything. Does a stream stop flowing when it comes upon a rock? Does the wind blow the leaves off only one tree?)

These two examples are how things of importance or great essence enter our lives.

A fundamental law of all living things. A natural order of life. A Pre-determined course of reality, constituted by Creation.

Only one today

I truly have given
everyway I know how
in all of my actions
that you will allow

        I've struggled in knowledge
        in logic and thought
        to tear down your barrier
        this wall that I've fought

I've hidden affection
when you weren't aware
not to push you away
from me, so I bare

        This hurt and involvement
        of love's tender touch
        and live in my prison
        called "I love you so much"

I've reached out my hand
when I thought you were drowning
for I stood alone
while life stands there clowning

        I've acted unwisely
        at times, this I've felt
        But the things that were done
        were with love's flowing help.

I've cried in the night
when you were so near
and my tears went unseen
because of my fear

                Why can't we see
                this wall that we share
                for we both want to give
                and we both truly care.

There are many tomorrows
but only one today
The longer we wait
in finding a way

                To freely express
                our faith in each other
                this idea man calls love
                that you are my lover

Time moves us away
lives drift us apart
our needs they surrender
to the hurts of the heart

                This reality can change
                let's show the world
                our love for each other
                flows natural, unfurled

That they may gain hope
from our interacting life
and we rise from the dust
of humanity's strife

> *For the children unborn*
> *we will build a foundation*
> *if together we project*
> *our love and elation*

in the truths we have found
by opening ourselves
to the love of each other
filling our own wells

> *There are many tomorrows*
> *but only one today.*
> *The longer we wait*
> *the harder the way.*

Returning

*As the snow melts in spring, bringing the
flow of water back to the dry stream beds
or creating new life flows so it was one
night in the souls of human beings.*

*Peggy . . . filled with excitement because of the
flowers Johnny had given her that day*

*Suzie . . . filled with deep emotion watching the tears
fall from the old man's eyes as he was filled with
the beauty of the art gallery confirming his
own sensitivity*

*Mike . . . filled with experiencing the young
people's sharing with each other*

Johnny . . . filled with everyone

*I was filled with hope that with sensitive
young people like these our future may become
a natural life flow.*

A special person

There was a special person
I always cared to know
for our lives would intermingle
no matter where we'd go

He was always just a shadow
or an image in my mind
or a faint and hazy memory
that life erased with time

After many years of wondering
a decision came my way
for I knew I'd have to meet him
and the time would be today

Without further hesitation
not knowing what I'd see
I looked into life's mirror
and met, who else, but me!

No longer was I lonely
For I liked what I had found
And began to open up to life
Not with words, man's empty sounds

But with actions I pursued
to express my inner self
with the people I encountered
gaining love, a natural wealth

I find I'm part of nature
so from nature I can learn
from the giants in the redwoods
from the hillside's lacy fern

As I walk through vegetation
everywhere I look
I see a part of me
in the leaves or running brook

In the butterfly's graceful motion
in the bird's delightful songs
in the movement of the little things
I feel no part of wrong

I feel no guilt with nature
nor does nature cause me shame
with it I feel as free as air
out there we're all the same

A man can become blind
if he continues to walk in the shadow
of his soul's own enlightenment

One's own discovery

I have become aware that a great majority of human beings were unaware of philosophy and logic and understanding and knowledge of their own soul. I found people seeing and feeling what others have told them, who in turn were told by someone else and so on. Is there no marvelous awareness of one's own discovery?

Giving

Love, like the sun, sends its warmth wherever you look. Though I know love is the center of which life revolves within our soul, as the planets to the sun, and can feel this truth within my own; sometimes I am left without understanding as one knows of a country where one has not been. This knowledge often alienates me from my fellow man. Often when I act upon my own conscience, I am condemned and misunderstood, thus my giving is not received.

The guide

If any of us are to become teachers, I believe a true teacher's gift, is to guide a man's discovery of himself. In truth we can only give what we have discovered for ourselves, freely and without intimidation.

Training

Thus I must travel in life, not vicariously, but I must master my own soul before I study the universe, for I believe there are universal truths that all men can live by entertaining harmony and balance. We must realize the precious consciousness of our existence, absorbing as much of life as we can, that the magnitude of our giving will become an inspiration to ourselves. Our mind gets sick without exercise just like our body. Our thoughts become stagnant unless they become actions. And we can only know good by training as hard in goodness as a champion trains for his sport!

Do good

*Who can do good without first knowing what it is
and how will it be found except through perception,
insight of God, in talking with a few truth seeking
friends, and by experiencing life. It will not be shouted
from the heavens, meaning the same to all who hear,
but by long learning of one's self and the causes of
ugliness and hate, by tempering of one's desires,
breaking down the barriers between people so they
find no need to escape, or use crutches and by loving
a human being with body and mind and coming into
submission to the truth. None of these things will
happen in a crowd but by relating to each person . . .
bending like a blade of grass before the wind of fear,
conditioning and prejudice for courage lies in our
ability to change, upon our own discovery.*

Index